A Grief Journal for Bereaved Parents

Other Books by Gussie Rose Press

90: A Conscientious Objector's Journey of Quiet Resistance
by Bruce Jay Wasser, Fern Schumer Chapman

Is It Night or Day? by Fern Schumer Chapman

The Sibling Estrangement Journal by Fern Schumer Chapman

Middle School Sleuths: How an 8th-grade Class Reunited Two Holocaust Refugees by Fern Schumer Chapman

Facing the Past: A Public Memorial Compels a Small German Town to Confront Its History by Fern Schumer Chapman

Three Stars in the Night Sky: A Holocaust Family's Odyssey of Separation and Reunion by Fern Schumer Chapman

Happy Harper Thursdays: A Grandmother's Love for her Granddaughter during the Coronavirus by Fern Schumer Chapman

The Return of Happy Harper Thursdays: The Guiding Light of a Grandmother's Love by Fern Schumer Chapman

Praise for *I Got Up*

"Brenda's story stands as a beacon of hope for bereaved parents and anyone who has sustained deep loss. She shows you that we can find meaning and connection even in what feels like unbearable circumstances."
— Genevieve Bryan

"Brenda Daly's *I Got Up* is a powerful and deeply moving narrative that intricately weaves together the complex relationship between traumatic brain injury (TBI) and addiction. As someone who has personally navigated the turbulent waters of TBI and addiction, this book spoke directly to my heart, resonating with my own experiences in a way few works have."
— Dave Closson

"Brenda's story is a deeply moving and poignant exploration of grief and loss. Writing about such a personal and painful experience requires immense courage and vulnerability. By sharing her story, Brenda not only honors the memory of her child but also opens a window into the profound emotional journey that parents facing similar tragedies endure."
— Mark Haydukovich

"...*I Got Up* is an insightful and profound journey about TBI, addiction, family and the bond between children and parents. I enjoyed the honesty and vulnerability of her writing; it allowed me to explore my own beliefs on these topics with greater compassion and consideration. Brenda does not shy away from the feelings surrounding life's circumstances. *I Got Up* is a valuable book for anyone wrestling with grief, loss, love and balance. I found healing."
— Nancy Lucas

A Grief Journal for Bereaved Parents

By Brenda Daly

Author of *I Got Up: A Mother's Story of Grief, Resilience, and Unending Love*

GUSSIE ROSE PRESS

A Journal for Bereaved Parents
Copyright 2025

ISBN: 978-1-962817-13-4 (paperback)
        978-1-962817-14-1 (ebook)

Welcome to *A Grief Journal for Bereaved Parents*

"Glad you are here. Sorry to meet you."

This is what I often say to parents at my talks who are on this unbearable journey.

I extend this welcome to you as well.

I'm sorry to meet you this way, and I offer my deepest condolences. You're reading this workbook, and that means that you are hurting, and my heart breaks for you. You have suffered the worst, most unimaginable loss: the death of a child. No matter the age, children are never supposed to die before their parents. It is not the natural order. Our children are a part of us, and, for a parent, the death of a child feels like the loss of a limb.

My sweet and loving son, Kevin, died suddenly and unexpectedly on October 21, 2018. Maybe it shouldn't have come as such a shock since Kevin had suffered a Traumatic Brain Injury eleven years earlier. He was left with physical, cognitive, emotional and social deficits, the least of which was chronic head pain and debilitating headaches.

Doctors prescribed many different medications to address Kevin's pain, including oxycodone. Sadly, as is often the case for many chronic pain sufferers, Kevin became addicted to the drug. When the medical community recognized that oxycodone was highly addictive, doctors began to cut back on prescribing these medications. For many patients with long term, unfixable, ongoing pain, this was catastrophic.

When he recognized that he was using more and more of the drug, Kevin decided to stop it altogether. His pain management doctor warned against this decision, saying that he would always suffer from pain and would need medication to function. His wife wanted him off the drugs.

However, stopping pain medication for six months only left Kevin in a chronic state of suffering; he would not feel the honeymoon of relief others experience when they stop drugs or alcohol.

One night, in desperation, Kevin bought one pain pill from an acquaintance at the gym, thinking it was safe. Sadly, it was a dirty pill containing a small amount of fentanyl that interacted with another medication he was taking at the time. The official cause of death – a drug interaction.

Since Kevin was living with me due to a separation from his wife, I was the one who found him dead in his bed. His death sent me into a tailspin of profound grief.

My background as a licensed clinical social worker for over thirty years did not help me cope with my horrific loss. I began to study grief. Currently, I hold three certificates in grief therapy and one in grief education. Both my personal and professional experiences are reflected in this workbook -- a companion to my book, *I Got Up: A Mother's Story of Grief, Resilience, and Unending Love*. However, this journal can be used as a guide to any kind of child loss, even if you haven't read the memoir, *I Got Up*. It is my hope that this journal will help you feel less alone, validate your experience, and educate you as you grapple with your mournful emotions.

Each of us grieves in our own way. This workbook is not a prescription for how to grieve; rather, it presents my lived experience and my journey through new understandings of this devastating loss.

I have found that writing can be therapeutic and an important tool in healing. Journaling offers an opportunity to sort through and untangle emotions experienced in grief, to begin to make sense of the loss. The questions at the end of each chapter provide a space to reflect on different aspects of your grief.

I offer you this journal to honor your experience in loss. Your story of loss needs to be told.

The workbook is divided into three parts: acute grief, functioning grief, and lingering grief. In acute grief, the griever experiences shock, disbelief, and unbearable, all-consuming pain. In functioning grief, everyday life becomes more manageable, although the grief is undiminished. As time moves on, in lingering grief, the pain is no longer all-consuming; however, this phase is marked by "grief bursts," which bring back the early, agonizing days of loss.

Grief is not linear. One phase doesn't necessarily follow the next, and the mourner doesn't move through the experience in specific time periods or stages. The process of grieving is fluid. However, certain identifiable characteristics mark each phase and offer some guidance. Instead of rigidly considering stages, it is more helpful to see the entire grief process as the repair of a Kintsugi bowl. This is the ancient Japanese practice of mending cracks and breakage beautifully, allowing the seams to show, revealing the damage while honoring the repair.

Table of Contents

Acute Grief

Acute grief immediately follows the loss of a child, and it can last from six months to two years. The circumstances of the death, your own relationship to the deceased, the type of loss, your support system and your emotional state and resilience are factors in your grief process.

Acute grief is described by the Loss Foundation (thelossfoundation.org) as "The early response to loss that can be intense and all-encompassing, it can involve intense daily yearning to be reunited with the lost loved one, significant emotional pain, as well as a multitude of physical reactions that many may never have been felt before (e.g. heart palpitations, butterflies in the stomach, frequent yawning, dizziness/fogginess), feelings of unreality. Frequently distracting thoughts of the deceased, trouble focusing attention, and forgetfulness. These are all **normal adaptive reactions** within the context of grief."

Each of us grieves in our own unique way, yet there are some common grief experiences. Grief can affect an individual physically, emotionally, and spiritually, disturbing the patterns of sleeping, eating, and engaging with others in the world.

Chapter 1
Disbelief

"Kevin's dead! Kevin's dead!" I screamed after finding him lifeless in his bed. How could that be possible? I just talked to him around midnight. He was fine. Now, in an instant, he was gone. Frantically screaming into the phone, I called other family members.

"Kevin's dead! Kevin's dead!" My disbelief and shock collided with shock and disbelief on the other end of the phone.

"Are you sure?" or "No, he's not."

No one could believe Kevin had died – least of all me, his mother. Suddenly my life turned upside down, and my brain was unable to process what had happened. I "knew" he was dead, but I simply couldn't accept reality.

Shock. Denial. Disbelief. Every morning, especially during the first year, I would wake up and my first thought would be *Kevin's dead*. Or I would gaze at his photograph hanging on the wall and say, "Are you really gone? You died?"

Still, I expected that at any moment he would walk through the door. Denial is this feeling that he was still just around the corner, and I had the impulse to pick up the phone and call to tell him about something, anything – and then having the devastating recognition, once again, that he had died. My brain was protecting me from the overwhelming pain of comprehending that Kevin was no longer here.

This feeling of disbelief can go on for a long time, maybe forever.

Anderson Cooper has said that, years after his brother Carter's suicide, he and his mother were plagued by painful, distressing ruminations about his death. They were both in disbelief. "It's inconceivable to me that my brother died in 1988 and I've lived more of my life without him than I have with him," Anderson revealed in an interview for People magazine. "It was the same with my mom. Till the day she died (in 2019)," he recalls, "we were both still stunned by what happened."

In her book, *The Grieving Brain,* Mary-Frances O'Connor, Ph.D., writes of how people experience utter disorientation in acute grief because the idea that a loved one is gone is outside the brain's experience. "The idea that the person is simply no longer in this dimensional world," she writes, "is not a logical answer to their absence, as far as the brain is concerned" – especially when the death is sudden and traumatic.

O'Connor explains this disorientation in relation to our attachment needs. The brain needs to know where a loved one is and how to keep him or her safe. The death of that loved one, as O'Connor states, is devastating for the brain, and it can take a long time to understand and accept the loss.

In what ways are you struggling with shock, numbness, and disbelief that your loved one is dead? Can you identify impulses, like picking up the phone or sharing an experience, that underscore your loss?

_____

_____

_____

_____

_____

_____

_____

_____

_____

_____

_____

_____

_____

What physical symptoms of grief are you experiencing? What triggers feelings of grief and disbelief most acutely? Explain why these moments are painful for you.

_____

_____

_____

_____

_____

_____

_____

_____

_____

_____

_____

_____

_____

_____

How can you begin to constructively process your grief? What steps can you take at this moment to support yourself during this acute phase?

_____

_____

_____

_____

_____

_____

_____

_____

_____

_____

_____

_____

_____

_____

_____

Is there someone in your life who you can talk to about your grief? Do you feel they understand your sense of loss and disbelief?

_____

_____

_____

_____

_____

_____

_____

_____

_____

_____

_____

_____

_____

Chapter 2
The Year Of Firsts

The 12-month period following the loss of a loved one is called the year of firsts. These 365 days without your loved one are acutely painful. Birthdays, holidays, anniversaries all come at you like a runaway train. But by far, the worst first is the first anniversary of the death of your loved one. This day is a definitive, dreaded marker that you have survived the year -- a feat you thought was impossible.

As I write in my book, ***I Got Up: A Mother's Story of Grief, Resilience, and Unending Love,*** Kevin's birthday came about a week and a half after he died. How were we supposed to get through that once-happy day when we were barely surviving his sudden death? We had to do something, so we acknowledged his birthday by releasing balloons into the air with loving notes attached (not a good idea environmentally, we later learned).

A few weeks later, Thanksgiving rolled around, with Christmas following right behind, just two months after Kevin's death. So many firsts in quick succession felt like an assault.

It was crushing to face holidays without Kevin. His absence left a gaping hole, not only in our hearts, but in all our celebrations. He had this big, larger-than-life personality. He *was* the party. Our firsts – birthdays and holidays – felt empty, flat, forced. We carried on for the children.

One thing I did learn during the year of firsts is that the anticipation and anxiety leading up to these important days can be worse than the day itself. Mounting anxieties can be overwhelming, as you fear you will come undone, unable to survive the loss again. When the holidays or birthdays finally arrive, those days may be surprisingly manageable.

Often, I braced myself for these difficult days, barely holding it together. Then, after the day passed, I would be hit hard by the pain all over again.

This poem captures the challenge of firsts and the eventual acceptance of the loss:

FIRSTS

By Becky Hemsley

*From the book **When I Am Gone***

People talk about the last times a lot.
The last time you said you loved them,
held their hand,
heard them laugh.
But what about the firsts?
The first time your birthday comes around and there is no card from
them.
Or the first time you gather as a group and they are missing.
The first time you wake up and remember they are no longer here.
The firsts will hurt in a way the lasts did not.
They will sting, burn, break you.
Because firsts signify the start.
A new beginning.
The beginning of the rest of your life
without them there beside you,
with a missing birthday card
a missing hand to hold.
The beginning of the rest of your life
missing them.
But remember…
We only experience something for the last time once.
And we only experience something for the first time once.
So I know you will miss them for the rest of your life.
But it won't always hurt or sting or break you
like this.

What feelings do you or did you have during the first year after your child's death? Can you describe a specific incident or experience that reflects some of those emotions?

_____

_____

_____

_____

_____

_____

_____

_____

_____

_____

_____

_____

_____

_____

How did you anticipate the first birthday or holiday, and how did you prepare or cope with the event? What were your emotions as you anticipated the holiday? What helped you to manage your anxieties?

_____

_____

_____

_____

_____

_____

_____

_____

_____

_____

_____

_____

_____

How did you feel after the holiday? Were you blindsided by grief that surged after the event?

_____

_____

_____

_____

_____

_____

_____

_____

_____

_____

_____

_____

_____

_____

Chapter 3
Photos

At Kevin's death, I felt an abrupt severing of our attachment. He was gone. His life was over. He wasn't coming back. The shock of the separation was so final.

"You can almost liken grief to an amputation," Dr. Ted Rynearson, author of **Retelling Violent Death** and clinical professor of psychiatry at the University of Washington, writes on SpeakingGrief. org. For me, it felt like I had lost a crucial part of myself.

I couldn't bear to look at Kevin's pictures scattered around the house. Two weeks before Kevin's death, I had pushed him to get family photos taken at JCPenney. The images capture a sweet, loving connection between a father and his nine-month-old baby boy. We decided to hang one of the two large photos in my house, low enough so my grandson, Mikey, could see them. On our living room bookcase, we placed a second photo of Kevin holding up Mikey, lovingly gazing into his eyes.

Then – Kevin died. I could barely look at those photos. It was simply too painful. I would glimpse those photos and think: "I was just talking to him 24 hours ago." Or 48 hours, or a week ago. Those photos marked the fault line in our lives.

I called my friend, a therapist who specializes in grief and loss.

"Paula, I can't even look at Kevin's pictures," I sobbed. "I want to take them all down."

"Don't do that, Brenda," she insisted. "Leave them up." She reassured me that she understood my pain and my desire to get them out of my sight. For some who are mourning the loss of a child, looking at the pictures and telling stories is comforting and healing. For others, it's simply too painful.

As grief shifts, feelings about the photos will evolve and transform. As Paula recommended, I didn't take the pictures down that first week. Yet, the pain was palpable – no matter whether the photos were hanging on the wall or standing on a shelf.

Five years after Kevin's death, those same photos that I couldn't tolerate now bring me some comfort. However, I still can't bear to watch Kevin on video. I recently watched a clip of him playing with baby Mikey, his shoulders moving up and down in his unique, full-bodied laugh. That laugh, a unique characteristic of Kevin filled with his life force and joy, made me miss him even more. The scene crushed me.

Others have the same deep emotional response to videos of their deceased loved one. Nicole Brown Simpson's mother said that, after her daughter's brutal murder, she could look at photos, but she could not watch her daughter talking on video.

The truth is, during that first year, *everything* will remind you of your loss. It might be a smell, a song, a restaurant, a show. Everything. And everyone will grieve differently. Grief requires us to find what works for us in healing: what we can bear, and for how long.

Avoiding thoughts or feelings is a universal response to emotionally charged situations, especially for those who are grief-stricken. Many grief-stricken parents avoid a deceased child's school, friends, activities they once enjoyed together, photos, and even the child's bedroom.

How do you feel about the photos of your loved one? Do they bring comfort or pain?

_____

_____

_____

_____

_____

_____

_____

_____

_____

_____

_____

_____

_____

_____

What does it feel like to see your loved one talking or laughing on video? Does that elicit a different feeling?

_____

_____

_____

_____

_____

_____

_____

_____

_____

_____

_____

_____

_____

As your grief changes over time, how have your feelings about photos or videos changed?

_____

_____

_____

_____

_____

_____

_____

_____

_____

_____

_____

_____

_____

Is there anything else that you can't look at? Any place you cannot go? What people, places, objects or experiences are you avoiding to suppress emotional reactions, and why?

_____

_____

_____

_____

_____

_____

_____

_____

_____

_____

_____

_____

_____

_____

What other areas in your loss require you to set firm boundaries in what you're able to see or do? Are you identifying and pursuing what works for you?

_____

_____

_____

_____

_____

_____

_____

_____

_____

_____

_____

_____

_____

_____

Chapter 4
Coulda, Woulda, Shoulda

Coulda, woulda, shoulda is a never-ending cycle of rumination in grief, especially when the loss is tragic or unexpected, as in the case of suicide or a drug overdose. However, parents of a child who dies of an illness may share the same feelings: *If only I had done something different.*

In *I Got Up*, I wrote: "I would relive the what-ifs and if onlys of all the decisions I had made from the day I found out I was pregnant to the day he died. I'd relive Kevin's childhood, examining it in excruciating detail. I'd search our entire lives together, sure I'd find the moment when I could have chosen differently.

"Through my studies, I have discovered parents who lose a child almost always feel guilt for not being able to save them. I've heard parents of children who died of cancer claim it was their fault, because they failed to get them to the doctor soon enough. Parents of children who die by suicide or drugs believe they could have somehow prevented it if they had just caught more of the signs.

"When a parent has a child die, it hardly matters the age, they will always look back with regret, believing they will uncover the moment they did something wrong. They do this because it gives them a sense of control; they want to fix it so they can rewrite the ending. Desperate to change the outcome, hindsight is a real tease, because following that path will only lead to abject hopelessness. Like a hamster on a wheel, the coulda-woulda-shoulda loop, is a never-ending cycle of rumination that will drive you mad."

As parents, we are wired to protect and care for our children. When we first hold our babies, an instinct emerges to do everything in our power to keep these innocent and powerless creatures alive. Even as parents of adult children, we continue to carry this belief that it is *my* job to keep my child alive. And when we "fail," we often blame ourselves. *Where did I go wrong?*

This is a recurrent issue for bereaved parents. It continues throughout the grieving process, but it begins in the acute phase, when the bereaved person is trying to make sense of what has happened. Phyllis S. Kosminsky and John R. Jordan write in the book, ***Attachment-Informed Grief Therapy:*** "…when a parent loses a child, much of the emotional pain endured by a bereaved parent has to do with the perceived failure to protect and nurture the child — ultimately, to keep the child from death."

These coulda-woulda-shoulda cycles of rumination make more sense in the context of neurobiology in the grief process. Our brain works to keep us safe. When we lose a loved one, our brain immediately searches for some way to control the outcome. "Psychologists call our thoughts about what could have happened *counterfactual thinking,*" writes Mary-Frances O'Connor, Ph.D, in ***The Grieving Brain,*** "Counterfactual thinking often involves our real or imagined role in contributing to the death or the suffering of our loved one. It is the million 'what if's' that roll through our mind: *If I had done this, he never would have died. If I had not done that, he never would have died. If the doctor had done this, if the train had not been late, if he had not had that last drink…*The number of possible counterfactuals is infinite."

Our brains search for solutions for two reasons. One is that, if we figure out why this happened and blame it on ourselves, then somehow, we can prevent another loss or future death from occurring. O'Connor suggests a second reason: "Our brain, by focusing constantly on the limitless number of alternatives to reality, is numbed or distracted from the actual, painful reality that the person is never coming back."

In fact, guilt actually serves a purpose, giving us a sense of predictability and control over the situation. It makes us feel the world is ordered – but *we* have somehow failed. The sense that bad outcomes occur for no discernable reason is simply too random to accept. Understanding my brain's need to control the outcome and rewrite a better ending to the experience of my son's death helped me to stop ruminating.

What are some of the what ifs and if onlys that cycle in your mind?

What do you wish you could have done differently? How has guilt defined your grief journey?

_____

_____

_____

_____

_____

_____

_____

_____

_____

_____

_____

_____

_____

Does your understanding of the brain's way of processing ease your grief path? What knowledge about the brain's workings helps you?

_____

_____

_____

_____

_____

_____

_____

_____

_____

_____

_____

_____

Chapter 5
Who Shows Up?

Often, we are shocked to learn who, in the darkness of grief, can and can't show up for us. The choices and actions of our relatives and friends can leave us reeling. Their absence can even damage our connection permanently.

When Kevin died, my sisters flew out the next day; my father and brothers and their wives arrived the following day. Friends and family brought over food and drinks. I didn't have to think about any of those daily demands.

In the early days after Kevin died, my circle of support provided a loving, safe space. I was deeply touched when one of Kevin's best friends drove from Arizona to California to express his condolences in person. His gesture -- driving thirteen hours straight to attend the funeral on Friday and then leaving right after the event so he could return to work -- proved that Kevin's life mattered and he was deeply loved. Relatives from different states came to honor him. We shared touching stories, comforted one another, and embraced each other as Kevin was lowered into the ground.

I had assumed, as I entered life without my son, everyone would still be loving and supportive of me. But some drifted off slowly. Some never showed up at all, saying it was too hard for them.

Everyone left. They returned to their own lives. For them, when the funeral ended, the event of grief was over. For me, it marked the beginning of my new reality. The sudden withdrawal of support stunned me, leaving me even more bereft.

Surprisingly, people I didn't expect to support me came through. Here is a strange truth of grief: Some people will be there for you through anything, all the hard days and difficult emotions. Some family and friends will disappear altogether. The loss of family members and friends compounds the grief.

In the book, ***It's OK That You're Not OK,*** author Megan Devine writes, "…it's one of the cruelest aspects of intense loss: at a time when you most need love and support, some friends either behave horribly or they disappear altogether. There are disappointments and disagreements. Old grudges resurface. Small fault lines become impassable distances. People say the weirdest, most dismissive and bizarre things.

"Grief changes your friendships. For many, many people it ends them… Your loss intersects with often hidden or especially painful heartbreak in the people around you. Your pain bumps up against their pain. We may not call it that directly, but that's often what's happening when people behave poorly or fail to understand the immensity of your loss. And even when your friends want to support you, we don't often have the skills -- no matter how skilled we truly are – to witness and withstand another's pain. Feeling helpless in the face of loss makes people do strange things.

"No matter what the deeper reasons are, the loss of friends you thought would stand by you through thick and thin is an added heartbreak. The injustice of these second losses makes grief itself that much more difficult."

Grief support groups sustained me. When friends and family couldn't fully grasp the devastating experience, other bereaved parents stepped in. Those who were enduring the same losses could witness my grief. I needed to feel heard and held by those who had walked this painful path.

In these groups, I found deep intimacy from shattering loss. Other grieving parents could empathize without words or explanation. The death of a child erases all barriers: race, religion, gender identity, political party. Nothing matters but the loss when you are sharing with other grieving parents. The loss is distilled to the purest emotions of love and compassion.

Who surprised you by showing up for you in your loss?

_____

_____

_____

_____

_____

_____

_____

_____

_____

_____

_____

_____

_____

_____

_____

Who has disappointed you?

_____

_____

_____

_____

_____

_____

_____

_____

_____

_____

_____

_____

_____

_____

_____

How do you think you would respond to a relative or friend during their time of grief? What emotions would their loss trigger in you? Would those emotions interfere with your ability to be loving and compassionate?

_____

_____

_____

_____

_____

_____

_____

_____

_____

_____

_____

_____

Have you found a grief support group that is helpful in your grief journey? What do you get out of these meetings and how do you feel after you attend one?

_____

_____

_____

_____

_____

_____

_____

_____

_____

_____

_____

_____

_____

_____

_____

In the circles, fill in the people and groups that represent who you depend on for support. Are there people who you can add to your circles? How would you like them to support you?

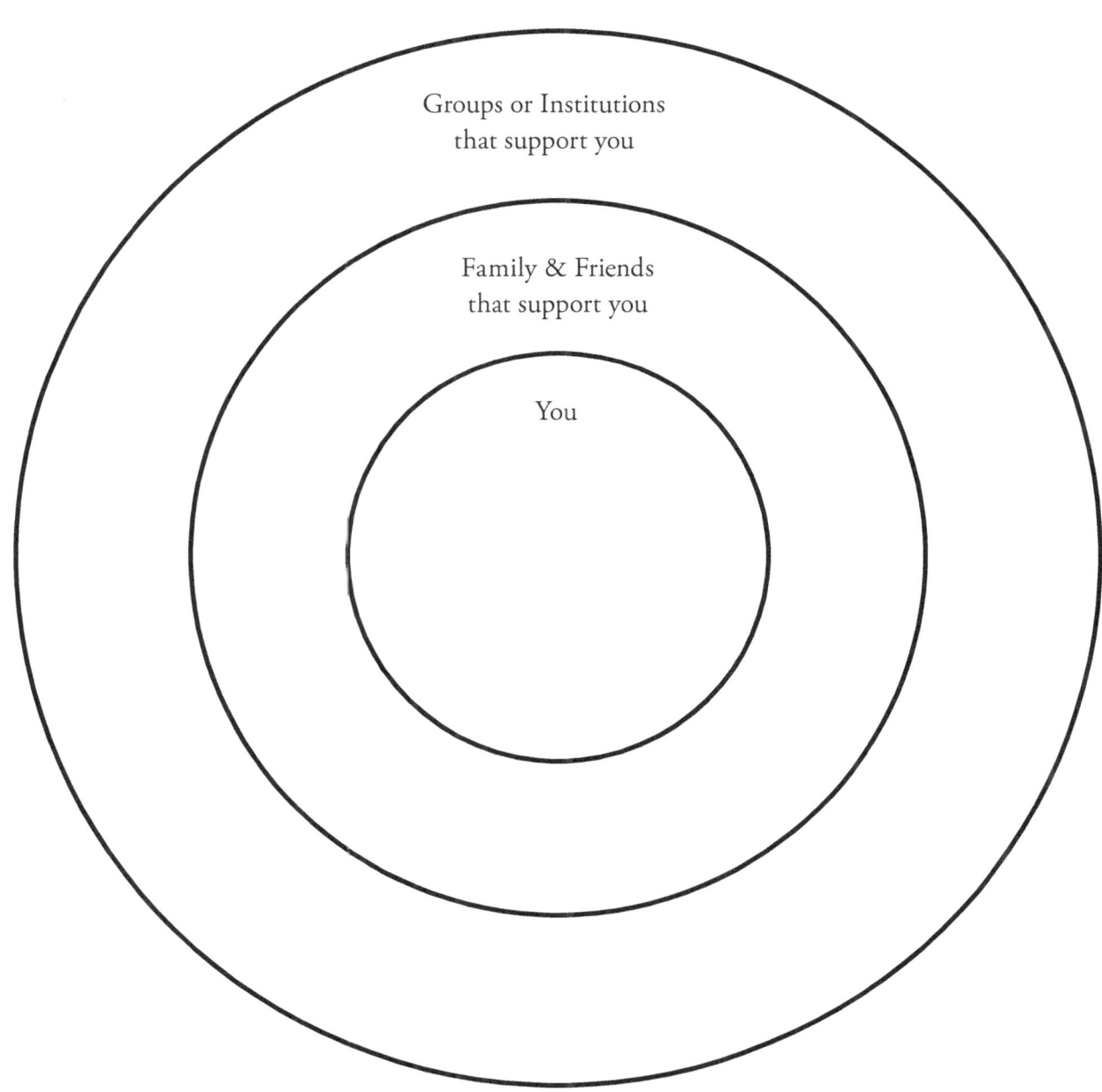

Groups or Institutions
that support you

Family & Friends
that support you

You

Chapter 6
Mirror, Mirror On The Wall

Catching a glimpse of myself in the mirror shortly after Kevin died was shocking. Who was that staring back at me? Hurt and anguish were etched into my face, and I was unrecognizable even to myself. I couldn't stand to see my pain; I had to look away.

I thought I was alone in perceiving that my face had changed. Then, I came upon Emily Listfield's article, "How My Skin Wore My Grief," in *Allure* magazine. Listfield described the changes in her appearance following the loss of two family members -- her brother died after a ten-month battle with cancer and, six weeks later, her elderly mother passed away. "I was left physically and emotionally depleted -- and it showed. My face had become gaunt and haggard, my sallow skin formed shadows etched beneath my eyes that no amount of makeup could disguise. Looking in the mirror only reminded me of what had happened."

Loss takes a toll on the body in a myriad of ways: high blood pressure, heart palpitations, difficulty sleeping, changes in appetite, a weakened immune system. Lack of sleep and continuous crying can lead to redness, swelling, and puffiness in the face and around the eyes. Not eating can result in rapid weight loss, leaving a hollowness in the cheeks that reflects the emptiness inside. Grief feels like a gut punch that may lead to digestive issues, such as nausea, stomach pain and diarrhea.

Another physical reaction to the traumatic loss of a child is the release of cortisol, the stress hormone, in the "fight or flight response." This can wreak havoc on many parts of the body, including the skin, possibly leading to a breakdown of collagen. A grieving person may notice deeper lines or a change in elasticity in the skin. Nobody told me I would wear my grief.

After Kevin died, even my hair changed. Chunks fell out. My stylist showed me the shocking amount of hair that came out on his hairbrush. Later, he told me that he had noticed the anguish on my face during the first year of my loss. When he saw these emotional and physical changes, he said his heart broke for me. He acknowledged my suffering without words -- through kindness and care.

Lack of personal self-care can contribute to issues with skin, hair, and teeth. Not surprising, personal hygiene often falls away in the acute phase of grief. In the weeks after Kevin's death, I could barely get out of bed. I didn't have the energy to brush my teeth or take a shower. I certainly didn't feel like moisturizing my face.

As I began to address my grief in therapy and heal from the initial blow of my loss, my appearance slowly returned to normal, and I began to feel like myself again. But it took time.

How are you wearing your grief? Be specific. How do you feel your grief has changed you physically and emotionally?

_____

_____

_____

_____

_____

_____

_____

_____

_____

_____

_____

_____

_____

How has your personal self-care changed as a result of your loss?

In your world, who gives you quiet comfort, as my hairdresser did for me?

_____

_____

_____

_____

_____

_____

_____

_____

_____

_____

_____

_____

_____

_____

Chapter 7
How Long Will I Feel This Way?

"How long is it going to hurt like this?" I cried out in the early weeks of grief.

Those shattered by traumatic loss often ask this question in the acute phase of grief when the abrupt separation is unbearable.

"It's a brutal, forced separation," writes David Kessler in *Finding Meaning.* The separation was so brutal that, for me, the world seemed to have fallen off its axis when Kevin died. I cried out for answers, pleading for some predictability and stability in this random universe. Give me a timeline and an outline of how to grieve. I demanded a map of the stages of grief. I need to know what's happening now and what's coming next. What is the path forward?

What I didn't understand then is that grief has a path of its own. I used to say it was its own beast – unpredictable, uncontrollable, unconquerable. In fact, there is no timeline. Despite the neat arrangement in Elisabeth Kübler-Ross's widely accepted theory of the five stages of grief, mourners don't move through her stages in sequence.

As Kessler and Kübler-Ross clarified in their book, *On Grief and Grieving:* "The five stages -- denial, anger, bargaining, depression, and acceptance -- are a part of the framework that makes up our learning to live with the one we lost. They are tools to help us frame and identify what we may be feeling. But they are not stops on some linear timeline in grief. Not everyone goes through all of them or goes in a prescribed order."

Grief, as I outline in this journal, falls into broad time periods – acute, functioning, and lingering phases. Even these, however, are not definitive. We move in and out of a range of emotions as we grieve. The acute phase is marked by shock, disbelief, and uncertainty, while other phases bring out different emotions. Even as the mourner integrates the loss, he or she may fall back into the overwhelming sadness that marked the earliest phase of grief.

The honest answer to "How long will I feel this way?" is that grief has its own trajectory. It requires the mourner to surrender to the process, fully feeling the emotions to process them rather than stepping away to avoid them. Avoidance only prolongs the grief journey.

As urgent as it felt to be released from suffering, I also feared what I'd feel if I did let go of the pain. This was my last connection to Kevin. The grief was all that remained of my attachment to him.

In *Finding Meaning,* Kessler describes the loss of his son. "I sat by his grave and told myself, 'This is where he is now,' even as I prayed to God, 'Please undo this.' I didn't know how to make it better. I didn't know how to live with it. At that time, the pain was my meaning, my only meaning. It showed me how much I had loved him."

Like Kessler, I wasn't ready to give that up.

What were your preconceived ideas about grief? Did you think the process was linear or staged? How have your views changed since the death of your loved one?

_____

_____

_____

_____

_____

_____

_____

_____

_____

_____

_____

_____

_____

_____

_____

How did you address your pain? Were these choices healthy or unhealthy?

_____

_____

_____

_____

_____

_____

_____

_____

_____

_____

_____

_____

_____

Kessler and I both experienced the pain in the early days as providing meaning or attachment. Did you find this to be true for your loss? Explain what has helped you move out of these limiting beliefs.

_____

_____

_____

_____

_____

_____

_____

_____

_____

_____

_____

_____

_____

_____

_____

Chapter 8
Shattered

Grief is a broken bowl. Kintsugi, the Japanese art of repairing broken pottery with gold paint, provides a beautiful image of how brokenness can be repaired.

The Kintsugi imagery represents my grief journey. In this first, acute phase of grief, the bowl or piece of pottery breaks, shatters, appears to be destroyed beyond repair.

"My world shattered into a million pieces on October 21, 2018, when my oldest son died suddenly and unexpectedly," I wrote in my book. I never knew if I would get up again. I never knew if I *wanted* to get up again. Getting up and moving on felt like I was leaving him behind, putting him in the past, betraying Kevin.

But slowly, I got up again. The next sections explore my rising: how I went from the deepest anguish to functioning in the world again.

Functional Grief

After the first year or two of loss, functional grief follows the acute phase. In the dual process model of bereavement developed by Margaret Stroebe and Henk Schut, two orientations emerge during mourning. One is loss; the other, restoration. Their theory describes an oscillation -- a movement back and forth -- between these two orientations.

The acute phase of grief is predominantly the loss orientation, when the grief is all-consuming. We focus on the loss; we yearn for the deceased; we may curl up in a ball in bed.

Slowly, we return to daily activities, basic hygiene, paying the bills, and grocery shopping. In this "restoration" orientation, we begin to pick up the pieces of our life and figure out how we will live without our loved one.

I remember clearly the first time I made a meal for my family, about a week and a half after Kevin's death. It consisted of a jar of spaghetti sauce, cooked ground beef, spaghetti noodles, and a bag of pre-made salad mix that included the dressing and croutons. To my astonishment, I successfully prepared a meal and set it on the table for my family – something I had done daily before Kevin's death. This was one of my first experiences in the restoration orientation. But, after dinner, I returned to my bedroom, feeling the weight of Kevin's death once again.

Chapter 9
Both/And

Early in my grief, I learned I would have to live in the "both/and" by holding two opposing thoughts and feelings in my mind at the same time. Kevin was gone *and* my sorrow was debilitating. *And* I had to take care of his baby son, my little grandson, who was only nine months old. I would be heartbroken, *and* the baby smiled, bringing me joy despite my grief.

Unaware of the disaster around him, Mikey, an innocent baby, was laughing. cooing, learning to walk, and eventually learning language. Witnessing his growth was bittersweet without Kevin, but I felt the joy of any grandmother as I played with my grandson. Mikey provided great respite from the grief.

The first time I heard myself laugh out loud, I was shocked by the sound that burst from my mouth. Guilt immediately ricocheted through me. If Kevin wasn't on this earth to enjoy his son, to experience these small moments of pleasure, then I shouldn't either. In time, after Mikey re-introduced me to small joys, I found myself laughing about something on television or something with my family. Spontaneous laughter.

One comedy show I liked appeared weekly on my YouTube channel. It was an antidote to the trauma, and I found myself anticipating each episode. For months, as I laid my head on the pillow every night, I was tormented by horrifying images of finding Kevin dead. Hours passed; I couldn't sleep. As I scrolled my phone in those lonely, midnight hours I came upon *"The Pete and Sebastian Show,"* which helped me to laugh again and lulled me to sleep. I began to experience both/and. Sorrow and laughter.

I also saw how I had changed at a few family gatherings. At my niece's wedding, four months after Kevin died, I was a shell of myself – numb, still in shock and disbelief. All I could do was show up. Silently weeping, I tried not to let anyone know how I was feeling. A few years later, when another niece got married, I was able to have fun, laugh, and dance.

Still, during certain songs or while watching the cousins dance together, I felt Kevin's absence deeply. Quietly, I excused myself from the party to wipe my tears. But I was able to return and enjoy the rest of the reception. Both/and -- I could be present at the wedding and sad that Kevin wasn't with us.

In her book, ***A Short Course in Happiness After Loss (And Other Dark, Difficult Times)***, Maria Sirois perfectly captured my experience at my second niece's wedding: "...step into the *and* of possibility. We can be shattered *and* heal. Hearts do break *and* grow in love and courage and capacity. Our pain may be excruciating *and* there is a way to live such that life shimmers with meaning and joy and we find ourselves laughing and dancing and celebrating even as we deeply miss what had been true."

When did you notice a movement from loss to restoration?

_____

_____

_____

_____

_____

_____

_____

_____

_____

_____

_____

_____

_____

_____

_____

When have you experienced living in both/and? Have you experienced two opposing feelings at the same time during your loss?

_____

_____

_____

_____

_____

_____

_____

_____

_____

_____

_____

_____

_____

_____

Describe a time (like my niece's wedding four years after Kevin's death) when you felt you stepped into the possibility of *and?*

_____

_____

_____

_____

_____

_____

_____

_____

_____

_____

_____

_____

_____

_____

Chapter 10
Before And After

While I was trying to find a place for myself in the both/and, I found myself split in two, living in the before and after of Kevin's death. A fault line defined my existence: Kevin was here, and then he was gone. In *I Got Up,* I write: "After is not just the empty place at the table or the text messages that no longer come. It's not just the "I love you" that will never be said again, or warm embraces that will never be felt. A whole person is gone from your life. And the hole is so big, it splits you in two; you become a before and after as well." Joan Didion explains in *The Year of Magical Thinking*: "… when we mourn our losses we also mourn, for better or worse, ourselves. As we were. As we are no longer. As we will one day not be at all."

I mourned Kevin, and I mourned who I was when Kevin was alive. My son was a part of my identity. We were attached. So, the question begs to be answered: Who am I now?

Author Ted Rynearson, M.D., a clinical professor of psychiatry, describes grief as a rite of passage on the website Speaking Grief (www.speaking grief.org): "There are really only two stages of grief—there's who you were before and who you are after. It changes us, and it's nothing we ever get over. I think it's something we carry forward forever."

Or, as a fellow bereaved mom once told me: "I died the day my son died. I'm not that person any longer. She's gone."

BEFORE AND AFTER

by Donna Ashworth

You may find that you begin
to measure your life
before
and after
they left.

And that's okay.

Just be sure
whatever you do
whatever tiny grain of strength
you have left
that you strive
to fill up the after
as richly
and as beautifully
as they helped you fill
The *before.*

The before
is committed to memory now
but the *after*
is totally up to you.
Make it count.

How did your identity and the way you see yourself change after the loss of your child? Who are you now?

_____

_____

_____

_____

_____

_____

_____

_____

_____

_____

_____

_____

_____

Can you identify and describe the before and after in your grief journey?

_____

_____

_____

_____

_____

_____

_____

_____

_____

_____

_____

_____

_____

_____

How will you make your after "count"? What changes will you make as you move forward?

_____

_____

_____

_____

_____

_____

_____

_____

_____

_____

_____

_____

_____

Chapter 11
Secondary Loss

When a loved one dies, you don't just lose that person. Like a rock being thrown into a pond, grief ripples through our lives and causes other casualties that are called secondary losses. For example, losing someone who held a role in the family -- such as mother, parent, father, sister, brother, husband -- is a secondary loss. We have lost the person we loved and the person who uniquely held that role.

Financial consequences also are common when the deceased relative contributed to the household, possibly forcing the sale of a home or a move to a less expensive apartment. A griever may be so devastated that he or she can no longer hold a job, derailing a career and drastically reducing earning power.

Another secondary loss may be the loss of a friendship or confidant, especially the relative who has died. In losing Kevin, I lost a deep connection with someone who helped me see and understand difficult situations. He had a rare gift of perception. I loved our conversations, and I will always miss him and his rare insights.

For a parent, another loss is the alteration of the family unit. The loss of an only child profoundly alters the family, however, the death of a child in any family redefines and realigns each member as well as the entire system.

Kevin's larger-than-life personality filled an immense space in our lives. Losing that left a deep void.

A year after Kevin's death, a friend lost her son to suicide. "We used to be a family of seven," she says, "and now we are missing one." Even in her large family, losing one child upset the entire family constellation.

Those who offer condolences sometimes say reassuringly, "At least you have other kids." Or, when a family has lost a baby, some say, "At least you can have another child." These words are not comforting. There is no replacement for the person who has vanished from life, as no one can take the place of a unique individual.

An unexpected, but significant and common, secondary loss is how grief affects religious beliefs. For me, I felt abandoned and rejected, and it seemed God didn't hear my prayers. He was no longer there for me. Why didn't God stop Kevin from dying? If God was all-powerful, how could he want me to suffer like this? How could I believe in God after what I've experienced?

Again, some who offer condolences come up short, as their well-meaning, spiritual platitudes fall flat. They often say things like *"God needed another angel."* Or *"God never gives you more than you can handle."*

This "spiritual bypassing" avoids uncomfortable feelings of loss, creating a safe distance between the bereaved parent's experience and the reality that anyone could lose a loved one at any time. It gives the erroneous impression that each of us has some control, and it supports the fallacious idea that "everything happens for a reason." There is no reason my son is gone while your children celebrate Thanksgiving with you. These comments undermine grievers, who desperately need their grief witnessed.

For my entire life, my faith was deeply knitted into my being. It anchored me. However, after Kevin's death, my faith became *another,* separate loss that I needed to grieve, sadly leading to other, tertiary losses.

When a mourner no longer engages in organized religion, he or she loses a faith community and its circle of supportive friends. Routine faith practices become difficult or forced when the words feel hollow. Clergy who don't understand the grief process often encourage grievers to "move on" and explain the loss as "God's plan." This may be true, but it offers no comfort.

Finally, one of the biggest losses for a grieving parent is the sense that we live in a predictable, secure world. A common fear is *"Will I lose you, too?"* This question underscores the loss of the assumptive world – the strongly held beliefs and ideas that help us feel safe and secure.

We assume our children will outlive us as that is the natural order. We believe that if we are good, loving parents, then our children will survive and live well into old age. The loss of the assumptive world turns grieving parents upside-down. Nothing feels right or true anymore. The universe is random if a child can die young of illness, accident, suicide, drugs, murder.

"A terrible loss of innocence has occurred," explains Kübler-Ross and Kessler in **On Grief and Grieving**, "only to be replaced with vulnerability, sadness, and a new reality where something like this can happen to you and has happened."

Kevin's death was like a bomb that went off in our family, leaving bodies scattered everywhere. My grief rippled into other aspects of my life – my confidence, my hope, my friendships. My children and grandchildren suffered as I felt I couldn't protect them from the randomness of life. These feelings are not as intense now, but I continue to feel the hit from Kevin's death.

How has the death of your loved one altered your understanding of the assumptive world? What religious, personal beliefs were upended by the loss of your child?

_____

_____

_____

_____

_____

_____

_____

_____

_____

_____

_____

_____

_____

_____

Identify and describe the secondary losses you have experienced as a result of the death of your child.

_____

_____

_____

_____

_____

_____

_____

_____

_____

_____

_____

_____

_____

_____

How would you describe your assumptive world now?

_____

_____

_____

_____

_____

_____

_____

_____

_____

_____

_____

_____

_____

_____

_____

Chapter 12
The Goneness

After the year of firsts, an ongoing awareness set in; my son is not coming back.

He's gone.

Every holiday. Every birthday. Every special family event echoes with emptiness. When I drive by a restaurant he loved or go to his favorite pizza place, I sense his absence. I feel it when I scroll through the contacts in my phone and see his name that I cannot bear to erase. The loss is especially intense when I take his son to the first day of first grade.

This is what I call my son's "goneness."

Initially, all I could feel was the abrupt separation that hurt so deeply that words couldn't describe the loss. Many people tried to comfort me by saying, "Time heals all wounds." I didn't believe it then, and I don't believe it now. I resented it when people said that because the loss actually *distorts* time. A woman who lost her husband 20 years ago may feel as if it happened only yesterday.

Over time, however, I had a slow awakening: Kevin is always in my heart.

During the pandemic, I took an online class called *"The Science of Well-Being,"* taught by Laurie Santos, Ph.D., a professor at Yale University. Research shows the ideas we have about happiness are fallacious. Getting a better job, more money, or a better house do not bring a sustained level of happiness. Instead, it's better to focus on practicing various "rewirements" to increase well-being.

Santos encourages her students to engage in a practice for thirty days to rewire the brain. I picked one of her options – to write down five things a day I felt grateful for. It is not enough to simply state, "I'm grateful I saw my grandson today." Instead, she asks her students to explore and provide details as to why the experience elicits gratitude. For example, I wrote, "I'm grateful I saw my grandson today because we played checkers and had so much fun laughing together. It was a sweet interaction."

In the first year and a half after Kevin died, I had no feelings of gratitude. In fact, I would have screamed at the suggestion. *Gratitude? How could I feel anything but loss since my son is dead?*

Two years after Kevin's death, I could identify a few reasons to be grateful. Nonetheless, as the exercise wore on, I had a harder time thinking of things to write about. One day, sitting in my living room, I looked out into my backyard and noticed a beautiful fuchsia flower. I went outside to get a closer look at the vibrant flower. To my surprise, when I looked up at the trees, I was struck that the leaves of the trees were so *green*. High definition. In living color. After Kevin died, I could not see color; everything was black and white. This observation made my gratitude list that day.

Practicing gratitude has helped to make me aware of the world around me and to open my heart to my ongoing love for Kevin. My deep feelings for him have survived and are palpable. His death did not rob me of my love. In fact, my love for him has only intensified. Those feelings of "goneness" have mitigated with this discovery, and I have a measure of peace: He may be physically absent, but he is still with me...always.

"When is it time to move into the love?" asks David Kessler in **Finding Meaning**. "When you feel that you have fully felt the pain. Even when you do, it will hurt again. It will just hurt less, and less often. Moving into the love begins with realizing the love was always there. It was there in the good times, in the illness, in the death, and in the grief. It was never absent, even in the worst moments, and it is there still. Death is not strong enough to end love."

How did you experience "goneness" after the death of your loved one?

_____

_____

_____

_____

_____

_____

_____

_____

_____

_____

_____

_____

_____

_____

_____

Did you experience a turning point in your grief that led to a sense of peace? How did it change your outlook on your loss?

_____

_____

_____

_____

_____

_____

_____

_____

_____

_____

_____

_____

_____

Write down five things you are grateful for and elaborate on each one.

_____

_____

_____

_____

_____

_____

_____

_____

_____

_____

_____

_____

_____

_____

In "The Science of Well-Being," Laurie Santos also recommended physical exercise, meditation, and practicing random acts of kindness as ways to increase your sense of well-being. Can you select one and begin the process of leaning into well-being?

_____

_____

_____

_____

_____

_____

_____

_____

_____

_____

_____

_____

_____

_____

Chapter 13
Who Am I Now?

"A profound loss changes us profoundly," Hope Edelman writes in *The AfterGrief: Finding Your Way Along the Long Arc of Loss.* "How could it not?"

A parental role deeply defines who we are. When a child dies at any age, we are transformed.

One of the most awkward questions after the death of a child is: "How many children do you have?" I never know what to say. If I tell the truth and say, "I have three children," that statement often leads to other uncomfortable questions. "Oh, where do they live?" or "What do they do for a living?"

Replying candidly, "My oldest is in heaven," is a conversation stopper. Our culture resists any discussion of death, especially when it's a child. Instead, to mitigate the discomfort in the conversation, I talk about my other children.

But I don't feel that's an authentic answer either. I'm still Kevin's mother! I didn't stop being Kevin's mother when he died. In denying Kevin's existence in conversation to accommodate others, I feel like I'm betraying Kevin.

Parents who lose a child to death constantly swim in these muddy waters, as they shift their identity to fewer children in an altered family.

"Catastrophic loss is like undergoing an amputation of our identity," writes Jerry Sittser in *A Grace*

Disguised: How the Soul Grows through Loss. "It is not like the literal amputation of a limb. Rather, it is more like the amputation of the self from the self."

In ***I Got Up,*** I write: "Billy Bob Thornton best described long-term grief in an interview he gave about living with the loss of his brother by explaining, 'There's a melancholy in me that never goes away. I'm 50 percent happy and 50 percent sad at any given moment.' I understand that on a level that I cannot explain. Before, I was whole in some way; 100 percent happy when I was happy, 100 percent sad when I was sad. Now, I'm never 100 percent of anything. And the funny thing is, you don't know you are whole until half of you goes missing. I'll never be the same again."

Sittser's book elaborates on this idea: "This crisis of identity, however, can lead to the formation of a new identity that integrates the loss into it. Loss creates a new set of circumstances in which we must live. When, at the right time, we are able to acknowledge the ineradicable nature of those circumstances, we can begin forging a new life for ourselves."

Who am I now? Each parent who loses a child must confront this question. I'm still answering it. I can say I'm more human. I appreciate that life is finite. My relationships with others, which were always important to me, have a deeper connection. Material things, never a main priority in my life, have even less meaning. I focus more on my inner life. Finding myself among all types of people in bereaved support groups, I'm less judgmental, less focused on the external, and drawn to the interior. I connect with others in all our brokenness – our common humanity.

How do you answer this question: "How many children do you have?" What feelings do you have when you give your response?

_____

_____

_____

_____

_____

_____

_____

_____

_____

_____

_____

_____

_____

How does Billy Bob Thornton's statement about being 50% happy and 50% sad at any moment relate to your grief? Can you understand the melancholy that never goes away?

_____

_____

_____

_____

_____

_____

_____

_____

_____

_____

_____

_____

_____

_____

_____

After the death of your child, who are you now? How does that compare to who you were before the death?

_____

_____

_____

_____

_____

_____

_____

_____

_____

_____

_____

_____

_____

_____

Chapter 14
In Grief, Men Are From Mars, Women From Venus

Spouses who have lost a child often expect their partner will grieve in the same way they do. However, men and women respond differently. In fact, parents, siblings, grandparents, aunts, uncles, cousins, even friends and coworkers will feel the loss in their own unique ways.

Many who grieve are not recognized. For example, sibling loss is often overlooked. My son and daughter were surprised when friends frequently asked, "How is your mom?" This comment minimized their grief, as if the death of a brother isn't as devastating as the death of a son.

Teenagers and children may seem like they are not suffering or grieving, but each developmental stage is characterized by its own understanding of loss. For example, young children cannot fathom that their loved one is not coming back. A teenager may not want the pain of grief to interfere with their social life, and they don't want to be perceived as different from their peers. But that doesn't mean they didn't love the person who died.

In my marriage, I quickly recognized that my husband's grief was different from my own. First, Kevin was my biological son; I had him when I was young, and we had been through a lot together, long before I married my husband. John came into Kevin's life when he was in high school. However, John and Kevin spent many years bonding over sports and even working together, growing close throughout the years.

My grief was raw; I felt exposed. Some days, I found it difficult to get out of bed. But John returned to work and distracted himself from his pain through action and services – such as transporting people from and to the airport when they came for the funeral. I was desperate to find others who could relate to my loss, and I sought out bereaved parents' support groups for solace. My husband didn't want to talk about his pain or about Kevin; therefore, he had no interest in support groups.

We gave each other the gift of grieving in our individual ways. I'm sure it saved our marriage. Grief is a personal journey and, ultimately, we mourn alone.

"Do Men and Women Grieve Differently?," an article on Legacy.com, recognizes the individual grieving paths of spouses. "Often when a husband and wife are grieving at the same time," it states, "one will think the other is not feeling the same depth of pain because the outward expressions are different."

In fact, research indicates that there are "male" and "female" models of grief. In the male model, according to the Legacy.com article, men want to return to their work or activities quickly and get on with life. They keep their grief to themselves and resist losing control of their emotions in front of others. In general, they don't like to ask for help.

In the female model of grief, women tend to express themselves, talking openly to others about their feelings. They will reach out to one or more people, rather than keeping to themselves.

The models are fluid, however. A female may behave within the male model of grief or a male may express his grief under the female model.

Identifying the male model and the female model of grief, how do you think you process your emotions?

_____

_____

_____

_____

_____

_____

_____

_____

_____

_____

_____

_____

_____

_____

How do you grieve differently from your spouse? How do you feel about those differences? Did you expect that your grief journeys would be the same?

_____

_____

_____

_____

_____

_____

_____

_____

_____

_____

_____

_____

_____

Consider how your other children have grieved the loss of their sibling. Your own grief is overwhelming, but it's important to remember others in the family are suffering, too. How are you able to support them on their journey? Have you explored their experience with them?

_____

_____

_____

_____

_____

_____

_____

_____

_____

_____

_____

_____

_____

Chapter 15
Holidays

At the holiday table, one chair now sits empty, and no one can ignore the presence of that absence. Bereaved family members feel the loss acutely at the holidays the family typically celebrates.

How do I deal with the holidays without my child? In a word: differently.

After Kevin died, I tried to maintain the holiday rituals for the sake of my children and grandchildren. But a bright light was gone, and we simply didn't feel like celebrating.

I remember walking out the front door – just one month after Kevin's death – and seeing our neighbor's Christmas light extravaganza on display. Given the world we were living in, it felt like a personal affront, a gut punch, a stab into my broken heart. The neighbors kept the "happy" display up until after the New Year.

I hated the lights, the carols, the words "merry and bright" that surrounded me wherever I went. I could barely catch my breath from Kevin's death. Somehow, I managed to get through the holiday by avoiding the mall and Christmas gatherings.

On Christmas day, my shrunken family got together for the kids to open gifts and eat a meal together. Yet, I felt numb and empty, a shell of myself. I pushed through the day, but finally collapsed on my bed in the evening, emotionally and physically drained. Lying there, I wondered, would I ever overcome the darkness?

Suddenly, my phone dinged. Two friends had sent separate messages that said the same thing: "I'm thinking of you."

When my friends reached out to me, I knew they understood my suffering – the pain of that night. Their compassionate, heartfelt gesture broke through my isolation. Their kind words were a lighthouse flashing hope and promise for me, illuminating a path out of the darkness.

Over the years, I've discovered different ways to navigate the holidays. First, I learned that it's okay to cancel traditional gatherings. I was grateful to have that option.

The next lesson I learned is that I don't have to stay long at holiday parties or gatherings. I have a choice: I can leave whenever I want, without fanfare, when I have reached my limit. I simply tell the hostess my issue and take my leave. In grief, I needed to recognize and respect my personal limits. I learned to pay attention to my body; it would alert me to when I had had enough. I found that the hostess always understood.

I, like others who have lost a child, altered decades-long traditions. One woman, for example, who lost her son around Christmas, arranged to go on a cruise in December every year to avoid triggers. To her surprise, the decorations on the cruise ship didn't bother her, though decorating her home without her son was unbearable.

I, too, became mindful of what I could tolerate. That first year, I attended a Christmas candle-lighting ceremony for bereaved parents, but it was not right for me. While others find this type of holiday event brings them peace, I found it to be torture. The event featured a montage of our children's photos, and I was crushed to see Kevin's recent picture among others that were old, dated, and faded. At that moment, I realized that Kevin would always be frozen in time. Even though the photo was barely three months old, he was already a memory. He would never grow older than the image of him as a 41-year-old man.

In time, I recognized that I needed to skip the candle-lighting events for bereaved parents. Instead, I attend a service at my church where I say prayers, decorate an ornament, and hang it on the Christmas tree at church. I established a new ritual: Each year I take the ornament back to the service and place it on the tree. We say prayers as we remember our loved ones. Spending dedicated time focusing on Kevin during the holidays brings me comfort.

Hard as it was, I realized that I wanted to put up a tree every year for my grandchildren. Even though part of me wanted to lie in a heap on the floor, I felt a need to show them life goes on. But, at the same time, I wanted to acknowledge that Kevin *had* lived; he was here on earth with us for a time.

I had carefully saved decorations my children had made in elementary school or Cub Scouts and putting them on the tree was a family tradition. Everyone in the family looked forward to seeing their handmade ornaments featured on our tree. Each year, however, it is bittersweet to hang Kevin's ornaments. The holidays are a challenge for living in "both/and" – grieving and healing.

Another new holiday tradition we established is to say a prayer as a family to remember Kevin. I place four votive candles, in Kevin's favorite shade of blue, near his picture. Then, each child reads a part of the prayer.

This prayer, called *"The Holiday Memorial"* and attributed to Sherry L. Williams, reminds us that Kevin loved and was loved. He was human – with all his strengths and shortcomings – and, with him, we felt the full range of human emotions. We didn't have perfect relationships or perfect love, but our love for Kevin was complicated, and vulnerable, and *real*.

The prayer also reminds us that Kevin is always with us: his unique sense of humor, the joy he brought into the world. This prayer helps us to remember that we continue to celebrate him and grieve our loss.

Here is the version of the prayer I modified for my family. Someone lights the candle, and someone reads what each candle represents.

"A Holiday Memorial for Kevin"

"As we light these four candles, we light one for our grief, one for our courage, one for our memories, and one for our love.

"This candle represents our grief. The pain of losing you, Kevin, is intense. It reminds us of the depth of our love for you.

"This candle represents our courage -- to confront our sorrow, to comfort each other, to change our lives.

"This candle is in your memory, Kevin -- the times we laughed, the times we cried, the times we were angry with each other, the silly things you did, the caring and joy you gave us.

"This candle is the light of love. As we enter this holiday season, day by day, we cherish the special place in our hearts that will always be reserved for you. We thank you for the gift your living brought to each of us.

"We love you, Kevin.

"Amen."

What holiday events do you feel you can't attend? What do those events bring up for you?

_____

_____

_____

_____

_____

_____

_____

_____

_____

_____

_____

_____

_____

_____

Identify how you can set boundaries around holiday parties and family gatherings to take care of yourself. Most hosts are understanding. What words can you use to explain your feelings to the host in advance of the event?

_____

_____

_____

_____

_____

_____

_____

_____

_____

_____

_____

_____

_____

How have your holidays changed since you lost your child? What ways do you remember your loved one? What new traditions have you implemented to survive and even celebrate the holidays?

_____

_____

_____

_____

_____

_____

_____

_____

_____

_____

_____

_____

_____

Chapter 16
Reassembled

In the functional period of grief, when the griever moves from loss to restoration, the Kintsugi bowl, broken into a million pieces in the acute phase of grief, is reassembled. I actually made a Kintsugi bowl from a kit. I laid out all the broken pieces on a table and figured out how they fit together, trying to sort out *who I am now*. How do I reassemble the fractured pieces of my heart?

I tackled the task like a puzzle, first attempting to glue the larger pieces together. The weight of the larger pieces, however, was too much for the glue to hold. When the pieces came apart, I had to gently hold them in place until the glue dried.

In reassembling life after loss in the functional stage of grief, I found I had to be patient, show the bowl tenderness, and provide support. Time and time again, I had to reassemble my broken places until the pieces finally stayed together. I had to give myself grace.

Lingering Grief

Grief never ends. The loss of a loved one defines us long after the acute phase of grief. Over time, however, the pain will decrease in duration and intensity. David Kessler insists that grief lasts as long as love lasts – which is forever.

Right after Kevin died, I couldn't listen to any music because it stirred up deep emotions and sent me into a downward spiral. Now, I can listen to music, but when I'm in a grocery store and unexpectedly hear even a note of music that triggers my grief, I descend into the acute phase of loss again.

I am more resilient now. Even though the feelings are deep and overwhelming, the grief won't last long, and I can recover more quickly. Sometimes, only an hour after those intense feelings, I find myself laughing on the phone with a friend.

In the early stages, grief felt like an ever-present hand covering my face that interfered with my ability to connect to others and blocked my view of the world. When asked how I was doing, I would always answer, "I'm fine." The hand of grief prevented me from stating my feelings honestly and being present in every conversation. I feared that if I exposed my sadness, it would overtake me again and I would never be able to crawl out from that abyss.

Now, five years later, the hand no longer covers my face; instead, grief is a constant companion standing next to me. I acknowledge that it's there: "Oh, it's you. I see you, and I'm right here with you."

Chapter 17
Grief Bursts

Sometimes, on a sunny day, a cloud appears out of nowhere, and a downpour of rain drenches the exact spot where you are standing. The deluge is shocking and bewildering; only a minute ago, there wasn't a cloud in the sky, and you were dry, standing in the same spot.

That's what a grief burst feels like. Just when I felt that I was functioning well again and managing my emotions, a sudden, intense wave of grief -- a tsunami of emotion -- would knock me over. Helpless, I was stunned again by the intensity of my loss. Years of grief therapy, attending bereaved parents' support groups, and researching the grief process did nothing to combat these deep responses.

One day, after hearing triggering music, I bolted out of the grocery store and sat in my car, weeping. I had no idea that my emotions were so close to the surface. Yet, there I was once again -- bereft, disoriented, bewildered -- wondering how I could go on living without my son.

These grief bursts are common in the grieving process. There is no way to predict or prepare for them, but fortunately they are temporary. Would I ever get over these horribly painful feelings?

Grief bursts are not a setback. They are just part of the process. "You have the right to experience 'grief bursts', Alan D. Wolfelt, Ph.D., writes in *Healing A Parent's Grieving Heart.* "Sometimes, out of nowhere, a powerful surge of grief may overcome you. This can be frightening, but it is normal and natural. Find someone who understands and will let you talk it out."

When has your grief caught you off guard? Describe specific situations that took you by surprise.

_____

_____

_____

_____

_____

_____

_____

_____

_____

_____

_____

_____

_____

_____

Identify specific experiences that trigger your grief bursts. Music? Places? Sounds? Smells?

_____

_____

_____

_____

_____

_____

_____

_____

_____

_____

_____

_____

_____

What feelings did you experience when you had your first grief burst? Fear, discouragement, hopelessness, helplessness? What did you do to mitigate these uncomfortable feelings?

_____

_____

_____

_____

_____

_____

_____

_____

_____

_____

_____

_____

_____

_____

Chapter 18
I Hung On

Ordinary People, a powerful film that came out in 1980, captures a family struggling to cope with grief after the loss of one of their beloved sons. Each family member is siloed in his or her own suffering.

While boating, the favorite son, Buck, has drowned. Conrad, who watched and survived the incident, can't stop blaming himself for his brother's death. Conrad attempts suicide and ends up in a psychiatric ward of a hospital. While in the psych unit, he befriends a young girl, Karen, who eventually dies by suicide.

Deeply distressed by the news of Karen's death, Conrad reaches out to his psychiatrist, Dr. Berger, and the two have a transformational conversation. The scene can be found on YouTube by searching for *Ordinary People (1980) Conversation with Dr. Berger scene.* Below is an excerpt of this powerful exchange between the psychiatrist and patient:

Conrad: Why do things have to happen to people? It isn't fair.
Dr. Berger: You're right. It isn't fair.
Conrad (crying): You just do one wrong thing and…
Dr. Berger: And what was the one wrong thing you did?
          You know. (Pause)
          You know.
Conrad: I hung on. I stayed with the boat.
Dr. Berger: Exactly. Now you can live with that, can't you?

Conrad (crying): I'm scared.

Dr. Berger: Feelings are scary and sometimes, they're painful.

This conversation illuminates Conrad's recognition that he is suffering from survivor's guilt over the loss of his brother. This type of guilt is common among those who survive an accident or an assault in war where one wonders: *Why did I live? Why did I make it when my friend did not?*

However, the death of a loved one can evoke similar feelings. I didn't think I had survivor's guilt; however, I knew I was riddled with questions of what if's and if onlys. I understood that I felt guilty about outliving my child. It was difficult to accept that I could be happy again without my son's presence. I'd have a good day and then feel I shouldn't; I limited my ability to live life and find enjoyment.

Five and a half years after Kevin's death, I started having intrusive, uncontrollable negative thoughts. These thoughts became so distressing that I decided to calm my anxious mind through neurofeedback treatments.

The therapy decreased my anxiety, however, it became clear to the clinician and me that these intrusive thoughts were stubborn and harmful. I was hurting myself, but why? The clinician helped me to identify the root of the problem: *"It's like survivor guilt, punishing you for being too happy, for being alive."*

In *How to Go on Living When Someone You Love Dies*, author Therese A. Rando, Ph.D., underscores this point: "One of the major stumbling blocks in resolving parental grief is the unnaturalness of a child's dying before a parent. This is something that most parents cannot comprehend. You expect that, as a parent, you will die before your child. The death of your child, therefore, is a death out of turn. It violates the cycle of nature in which the young grow up and replace the old. The very order of the universe is shattered, and this is something that you might not be able to make sense of. You may experience 'survival guilt,' the guilt that people feel when the one they love has died and they continue to live. Therefore, the death of a child is one of the very most difficult to cope with because it does not make any sense, it violates all expectations – even nature itself – and leaves bereaved parents feeling guilty for being alive."

This concept is at the heart of the movie, *Ordinary People*. Like Conrad, I couldn't overcome the fact that I was still alive and my beloved family member wasn't. I couldn't accept that he had died before me or that he had a tragic fall that left him with a Traumatic Brain Injury (TBI).

"It isn't fair," Dr. Berger says to Conrad. I felt the same way. Somehow, I believed that if I experienced happiness, I was a bad mother who didn't love her child as much as she thought she did. I had set up a twisted equation: if I enjoyed my life, I was accepting his death – which was intolerable to me. Intellectually, I knew this wasn't true, but my anxious mind punished me relentlessly.

Bereaved parents often have this belief. It's not just the guilt we have because we can't keep our child alive, it's the guilt that we have outlived our child, upending the natural order of the parent/child relationship. Our brains don't know what to do with this awful reality.

"Feelings are scary." Conrad's psychiatrist says. "And sometimes they're painful."

Hurt hurts!

Do you feel you have survivor's guilt? How does it manifest in your life?

_____

_____

_____

_____

_____

_____

_____

_____

_____

_____

_____

_____

_____

_____

_____

Explain how you've experienced scary feelings? What feelings are you avoiding? Does it feel like you will be consumed by the pain if you admit that you are grieving or that you are healing?

_____

_____

_____

_____

_____

_____

_____

_____

_____

_____

_____

_____

_____

_____

Do you allow yourself to feel joy? If not, why not? It's okay that you're not okay, as Megan Devine titled her popular book on loss, but is it okay if you *are* okay? Describe the mixture of emotions you feel as you heal.

_____

_____

_____

_____

_____

_____

_____

_____

_____

_____

_____

_____

_____

_____

Chapter 19
Does He Still Matter?

The fifth anniversary of Kevin's death would be a huge marker for me: it had been five years since I've seen Kevin, heard his voice, listened to his laughter. Five years since I told him I loved him or got a text message from him with his classic response, "I love you, buddy." In retrospect, I wonder if Kevin knew his time on earth was short because he never passed up an opportunity to tell family and friends how much he loved them.

My biggest fear for this anniversary was that no one would remember him. No one would think about him anymore. I feared he was no longer part of the memories of his family and friends. People would stop saying his name.

I knew that sitting around waiting for others to remember him on this day would only add to my grief. I needed to do something. I wanted to turn this deep sadness into something that served others.

In anticipation of the anniversary, I decided to do a fundraising event with *Shoes That Fit*, a charity that provides athletic shoes to children in need. I was committed to turning my pain into purpose. Kevin loved athletic shoes, and he also loved generously helping others. "Kicks for Kevin" raised money to buy athletic shoes for two schools in Winslow, Arizona – more than 550 kicks (pairs). This fundraiser honored both Kevin and me, and it truly turned my pain into service.

Throughout the campaign, I received donations from many friends and family members. My children watched closely to see who donated, and I sent off thank-you notes to let donors know how much it meant to our family that they still remembered Kevin. I'll never forget how my niece, Jenny, responded after I thanked her for donating. "Of course! He is still very loved."

Her words still make me cry. This is exactly what I needed to hear! She penetrated my sadness. Kevin was — is — still remembered. Still loved.

How do you feel about upcoming anniversary dates of your loved one's death? If you fear your loved one won't be remembered, explore that fear. What does that mean to you?

_____

_____

_____

_____

_____

_____

_____

_____

_____

_____

_____

_____

_____

What words or kindnesses from others penetrated your sadness?

_____

_____

_____

_____

_____

_____

_____

_____

_____

_____

_____

_____

_____

How can you turn your pain into purpose? What kind of service projects can you create to honor your loved one and keep his or her memory alive?

_____

_____

_____

_____

_____

_____

_____

_____

_____

_____

_____

_____

_____

_____

Chapter 20
Time's Up!

Time's up! "You should be over your grief by now." Certainly, you shouldn't be actively grieving after two years, or five years, or whatever time frame other people think is enough.

We live in a grief-illiterate society. People are woefully ignorant when it comes to understanding the grief process and how long it takes to heal. Not only does the average person lack an understanding, but professionals who work with death and bereavement -- doctors, nurses, members of the clergy, even therapists -- fail to understand the bereavement process when it comes to the death of a loved one. The idea that one should move through grief, and do it quickly – "get over it," or "move on," or "get back to normal" -- is pervasive in our society, even among the healthcare professionals we turn to for guidance.

Ours is a culture that avoids the topic of death. It's too threatening, too overwhelming -- so family, friends, and even therapists gloss over the griever's deep feelings and use pat platitudes that provide little reassurance or comfort.

When Kevin died, I was lucky to have a great therapist who listened, consoled me, and never pushed me to move on. Four years later, I visited a different therapist who specializes in trauma treatment, but she was quick to say, "It's been a long time; you should be in a different place with your grief."

On the fifth anniversary of my son's death, I was able to celebrate his life with my children and grandchildren. Instead of painful recollections, we shared warm stories about his life. We laughed and loved him again. It felt like he was right there with us. *We've come so far,* I thought.

When I shared this with my therapist, she was delighted and pronounced that I was now recovered from my grief. "Five years is usually the marker for grief ending," she said confidently. I was relieved that the fifth anniversary passed without too much family distress.

A week and a half later, on Kevin's birthday, I crumbled. *Thank God,* I thought, *I have an appointment with my therapist today.* I walked into her office, sat down and sobbed. "It would have been Kevin's 47th birthday today," I gasped. Shocked, she stared at me, confused that I had lapsed into deep mourning again.

"You don't like to be happy, do you?" she said.

I was stunned.

Her reaction showed me how little she understood of the non-linear nature of grief.

No, I thought, I'm *not* happy on my dead son's birthday. That seemed to me to be a legitimate, understandable reaction to this moment in time.

I never went back to her again.

As a clinician myself, I suspect that somehow, she felt my sadness reflected poorly on her therapeutic skills. My continuing grief made her feel like a failure.

There is no timeline in grief. In *"The Myth of the Grief Timeline,"* an article on the website, What's Your Grief? (www.whatsyourgrief.com), Eleanor Haley states that the idea of a timeline is a misnomer. "Anyone familiar with grief," she writes, "understands that associated feelings, setbacks, breakthroughs, roadblocks, triggers, and resolutions can occur at unexpected, unpredictable and inexplicable times and durations.

"Grief is not a race with a start and finish line, it's a labyrinth of twists and turns and dead ends. Grief is like trying to swim past the break in the ocean -- you wade in but every once in a while a wave comes up and knocks you back a few feet. You're still deeper than when you started, but not as deep as you were before the wave hit."

I learned to carry my grief, but none of us fully recovers from the loss. I was okay on the fifth anniversary of the death, but I was blindsided by the unpredictable wave of grief on Kevin's 47th birthday.

Grief never ends because the love never ends.

Did you have expectations that grief has a timeline? What were they? Do you feel like you have failed when you don't meet those milestones?

_____

_____

_____

_____

_____

_____

_____

_____

_____

_____

_____

_____

_____

Who in your life has suggested you "move on" or "get over" your grief? Write down these conversations. How did you feel in your body when you had these conversations, and how do you self-talk to resist that type of thinking?

_____

_____

_____

_____

_____

_____

_____

_____

_____

_____

_____

_____

_____

_____

How did therapeutic or healthcare professional people support or undermine your grief journey? How did those people make you feel? Were you able to pick and choose the appropriate people who could give you the support you needed?

_____

_____

_____

_____

_____

_____

_____

_____

_____

_____

_____

_____

_____

Chapter 21
Continuing Bonds

"We have a bond no one can break," Kevin would often say to me. We certainly had a bond -- a deep emotional connection that began even before he was born.

For me, it was spiritual and psychological, but it was also biological. In the birthing and nursing of babies, oxytocin – the "love chemical" that bonds us to our baby – is released in the mother's body. Even when a baby is adopted, these chemicals flood a mother when she holds the baby in her arms for the first time. Oxytocin also is released when we fall in love.

Human beings are hardwired for connection and attachment. It's biology, and we depend on it for our survival.

So what happens when someone we love dies? What happens to the connection? Grief cannot happen without attachment. Our grief is directly related to our ability to love. When there's no attachment, there's no grief.

Immediately after Kevin died, I felt our bond was completely severed. It felt abrupt. "The worst thing about death is that it is so final, permanent and unchangeable," writes Dr. Lucy Hone in ***Resilient Grieving: How to Find Your Way Through Devastating Loss***.

At first, every day I woke up and thought, *He's gone.* In time, as I began to heal, I realized my love for Kevin is fully alive – as if he were still here. My love for Kevin cannot die. In fact, my love for him has grown. It's consoling to know that there's a special place in my heart reserved only for him. I had not lost our time together, or our precious memories.

"We can continue to 'have' what we have 'lost', that is, a continuing, albeit transformed, love for the deceased," writes Thomas Attig, in ***How We Grieve: Relearning the World.*** "We have not truly lost our years of living with the deceased or our memories. Nor have we lost the influences, the inspirations, the values, and the meanings embodied in their lives. We can actively incorporate these into new patterns of living that include transformed but abiding relationships with those we have cared about and loved."

My life is filled with tributes to Kevin. I honor him in every group I lead, every talk I give, every workshop I host, every collage I create. I find myself caring for his son with extra love. I've funded a scholarship in his name to help recovering addicts in aftercare through the Herren Project. I've partnered with *Shoes That Fit* bringing athletic shoes to students at underserved schools in his honor. And I talk to strangers -- because gregarious Kevin never met a stranger. This is how I bring Kevin's unique, positive qualities to the world. We even honor and remember him by eating his favorite foods: pizza and chicken wings. I find Kevin everywhere.

As I often say, bring your loved one into the NOW. Say their name. Tell their stories. Laugh about the silly things they did. Plant a tree or create a garden in your loved ones' memory. Some people set up an altar with pictures and special mementos to remind them of their loved one. I wear a necklace with a K to feel Kevin close to my heart. Others wear bracelets or other pieces of jewelry. Writing letters to the deceased and having them "respond" using your non-dominant hand is another suggestion. I love collaging, especially creating a new book by using images and words on pages of an old book. My story, like the book, has been altered.

In this way -- in all these ways -- I connect and remember Kevin.

Your body is away from me,
but there is a window open
from my heart to yours.
Rumi

Identify experiences when you sense your loved one. Make a list of the places and things where you find him or her. Do these memories bring you comfort or pain?

_____

_____

_____

_____

_____

_____

_____

_____

_____

_____

_____

_____

_____

What stories about your loved one spark your love for him or her? When do you and your family tell these stories? Can you create a special time or place when you can feel the love and bond that continues to grow and change?

_____

_____

_____

_____

_____

_____

_____

_____

_____

_____

_____

_____

_____

_____

_____

How can you bring their influences, inspirations, values and meanings into your life now? What ways can you give purpose to your loss? What did your loved one bring into this world that you can intentionally share?

_____

_____

_____

_____

_____

_____

_____

_____

_____

_____

_____

_____

_____

_____

Chapter 22
Future Grieving

Lingering grief includes a future of loss, as we must go on without our loved one. Every occasion where they should have been present – graduations, weddings, births – is a wound as well as a joy because our loved one is absent.

When a family member passes the age Kevin was when he died, I see the future we all lost. I see things, too, the things they are missing. The loss is especially evident in my grandson's life; his first day of school is always bittersweet. Kevin, a sports fanatic, will never see his son play baseball or basketball or graduate from high school. He won't delight as his son trick-or-treats. He won't see his son open gifts on Christmas morning.

Best-selling author Donna Ashworth captures this chronic aspect of grief in real time in this poem:

THE LIFE YOU DIDN'T LIVE

It's the life you didn't live
that plays
like a movie in my mind
the places you didn't see
the people you didn't meet
It's the new home
you never bought
the new car
you did not drive
the holidays you didn't take
and the sea air
you did not breathe.
It's the laughs you did not have
and the friends you did not hug
the birthday candles
you didn't blow out
and the gifts
unwrapped.
It's the life you did not live
that plays like a movie in my mind
A movie I would give anything I own
to see take place
in real time.

Which occasions bring up your grief for the moments your loved one will never have?

_____

_____

_____

_____

_____

_____

_____

_____

_____

_____

_____

_____

_____

Chapter 23
I Got Up

In *I Got Up: A Mother's Story of Grief, Resilience, and Unending Love*, I write about how I moved from deep despair after the loss of my son to living in the world again.

The death of a child knocks you down, and it feels like you will never be able to pick yourself up off the ground. I titled my book, *I Got Up* because it is the only way to recover from such a tragic, untimely loss.

Resilience in this context is not the dictionary definition of bouncing back or springing forward or quickly recovering from something. Resilience in grief can best be defined by what it is not.

Resilience in grief is not:

Linear. We don't move from point A to point B. Grief is not a straight line. It's a messy ball of emotions like a tangled ball of yarn that's tied up in knots.

Staged, as Kübler-Ross has suggested. Grief is not about completing one stage and moving on to the next. It does not culminate in acceptance. Things never return to normal.

Finite. We never fully recover from the loss of our loved ones, even though periods of distress decrease in duration and intensity.

Easily rationalized. Everything that happens in life isn't about a lesson to be learned. Contrary to what many say, there is no silver lining in the death of my son, Kevin. Kate Bowler calls her book, ***Everything Happens For a Reason (And Other Lies I've Loved)***, because there aren't necessarily lessons or reasons for a tragic loss. Grieving is not a negative mind-state that can be rectified with positive thoughts.

Grief is a normal, natural process that occurs when we lose someone we love. It is not pathological. It does not need fixing. Grief needs to be experienced.

So, how did I get up again? What happened between being shattered and gluing myself back together?

"How do you mend a broken heart?" David Kessler asks in ***Finding Meaning.*** "By connection."

I found connection with people who witnessed my pain, sent loving messages, showed up for me with food, candles, or hugs. They fueled my resilience. A support group of bereaved mothers rescued me from the deep end of the ocean of grief. In turn, I was able to reach out to others and pull them to shore.

First, we rely on others. And then, in time, others rely on us.

Healing does not necessarily mean that you are improved by what you've endured. I have changed because of my devastating loss, but I didn't *need* to lose Kevin to develop myself. "I'm not a better person because of it, just a different person," Lucy Hone writes in ***Resilient Grieving,*** about post-traumatic growth following the loss of her daughter.

Part of me died the day Kevin died. I never thought I could live in the world without him. But, as I wrote in, ***I Got Up,*** with courage, strength and connection, ultimately, I got up.

What does resilience in grief look like for you – not in how our culture defines it?

_____

_____

_____

_____

_____

_____

_____

_____

_____

_____

_____

_____

_____

_____

Identify the ways in which you've changed as a result of the loss of your child?

_____

_____

_____

_____

_____

_____

_____

_____

_____

_____

_____

_____

_____

_____

_____

How did you get up from the devastating loss of your child and begin living in the world again? Who or what helped you to get up?

_____

_____

_____

_____

_____

_____

_____

_____

_____

_____

_____

_____

_____

Chapter 24
My Kintsugi Bowl

My Kintsugi bowl, which I made from a kit, has a hole. When it broke, part of the bowl turned to dust. The bowl was irreparable. But I like to see the hole; it reminds me that a part of me is missing. Both the hole and the bowl's mended cracks, filled with gold, represent my journey to restore my heart. I will always carry both – the heartbreak and the healing.

About the Author

Brenda Daly, Ph.D, LCSW, is a psychotherapist with over 40 years of experience. She is the author of ***I Got Up: A Mother's Story of Grief, Resilience, and Unending Love.*** The sudden loss of her son, Kevin, left her bereft and in search of a deeper understanding of grief and loss.

She holds several certificates in grief therapy and is especially proud of her certificate in art-assisted grief therapy. Through collaging, Brenda found her way to resilience in loss. Now retired from private practice, Brenda regularly conducts talks on grief and leads workshops on The Art of Resilience.